CW00747408

The Secrets of My Spectrum

Callum Knight

First published in Great Britain in 2019.

The author has asserted their right under the Copyright, Designs, and Patent Act 1988 to be identified as the author of this work.

ISBN: 978-1916258600 (print paperback)

ISBN: 978-1916258617 (eBook)

DEDICATION

For all those who seek to understand our differences without judgement.

Thank You!

CONTENTS

INTRODUCTION

Three years ago, when I was thirteen years old, I was diagnosed with autism spectrum disorder. It came as a shock to everyone in the family. We all knew I had problems with speaking up for myself and I didn't particularly enjoy interacting with other people, but everyone said I was shy, and I thought that was why.

Over the past few years, I have found life more difficult because I feel like more is expected from me, but I haven't caught up with those expectations yet.

Even just having a short conversation with someone can be difficult, because unless I tell them I have autism, they expect me to be like any other kid my age because my differences are not visible from the outside. In fact, from the outside, I look like any other sixteen-year-old, so why wouldn't they expect me to act like one? But the thing is, I don't feel comfortable telling people I have autism until I get to know them, because I don't want them to see me differently or judge me based on information which may not relate to me.

Usually when I do pluck up the courage to say I am autistic, people reply 'you don't look like you have autism.' At times I've even wondered if they think I'm lying to them, because often people don't understand autism, mainly because we are all different, and no two people with ASD present with the exact same challenges. When they ask me to explain what autism is, I have no clue how or where to start, and it makes me feel more vulnerable than I did to begin with; so, I decided to ask for some help to write this book. I sat down and thought hard about how I could explain my challenges and share my experiences in the hope readers will get a good insight into parts of the spectrum that affect me. Hopefully, you'll be able to use this knowledge as a tool to help identify triggers which may be present in your loved ones or people you know, and you will feel more able to support them when they're suffering or feeling out of control.

ASD is a spectrum, so we all face different struggles, but we do all need to feel validated, understood and accepted for who we are—without judgement.

'Look in the direction you're going,' my mum used to say. As soon as I started walking, I often walked into things, and my mum's hand would reach out and pull me away from whatever I was about to crash into.

I was a clumsy kid. I had a habit of running while looking behind me and yes, I face-planked into lampposts more times than I can remember!

Like most mothers, my mum took me to lots of kids' clubs when I was a toddler, but I refused to leave her side. She says she couldn't understand why at the time, but something told her to delay putting me into school, and she took a class at the local nursery in town which taught parents how kids learned to read and write.

Because it was a nursery, I was given free childcare while she took the class.

My mum said that day was her earliest recollection of me having a full-blown meltdown. I was around eighteen months old and I screamed the place down.

I enjoyed going to a gymnastics group when I was two because all the kids' parents took them around the equipment and I didn't have to interact with the other kids, but as I got older, the expectation was that we would go into the class by ourselves and leave our parents waiting outside. I refused.

My mum waited with me outside for a while to see if I would decide to join them later on, but while they played I sat with her and looked out the window, counting the cars going past on the road outside or looking for cars of a particular colour. I loved patterns and numbers.

COMMUNICATION

By the time I was four years old, I rarely said
more than a few words at a time. My speech was
limited until I was around six or seven, but as I
was home educated, I wasn't the only child who
didn't speak much in my social group. Everyone
at home thought I was just shy and quiet because
when I was a year old, one of the many classes my
mum took me to in the hope I would eventually
enjoy spending time with other kids was a 'sing
and sign' class. So, I knew how to use sign
language to ask for food, drink, and tell her if I
was in pain. At that time Mum said she thought I
wasn't talking because I enjoyed signing more

than I wanted to speak, and she didn't think much of it.

She continued to take me to groups, refusing to give up on me, and I was pretty neutral in classes and was seen as a polite, sometimes shy kid. I never really felt the need to be with other kids, so I'd join in for a while, but I was just as happy by myself. I made some good friends, but we didn't see each other every day. We got together maybe once or twice a month, which gave me enough time in between to recover from the interaction and enjoy the next time we were together.

I don't mind interaction as much on a one-to-one with someone I've had a chance to get to know.

When my brother got older, Mum took us both to groups outside of our usual group of friends and as long as we were together, we both had fun, but we refused to be separated.

My mum persisted and tried different interest groups, smaller classes, sports clubs and encouraged me to go and have fun with the other children over the years, but I found all the groups more and more difficult as I got older and eventually separated myself completely, preferring to spend time playing with my cars alone.

Even when my little brother joined in, I encouraged him to play alongside me, but I didn't want to play with him and he had to stick to my rules—everything had to be as realistic and true to life as possible. The traffic had to go the correct way around the roundabout, the cars had to be parked properly and if he tried to overtake me on a single road, I got cross. I loved jigsaw puzzles; and I really, really loved Thomas the Tank Engine.

I used to like testing my mum to see if she could remember all the names of the trains and delighted in her getting it wrong so that I could correct her. She knew I enjoyed it too, because she always got it wrong just so that I could.

The jigsaw puzzles were sometimes challenging, because I had no problem working out where the pieces fit, but it used to take me a while to physically place them.

Mum said she noticed that my hand-to-eye coordination wasn't great. I would wiggle pieces around for a while before fitting them in place, so she encouraged me to make things with Play-Doh or cut shapes out with different-edged child scissors to help me gain more manual control. That was fun too, I'd spend ages making things with Play-Doh.

It's difficult for me to put my feelings and thoughts into words, whether through conversation or written down on the page. It takes a long time to process my emotions because they're in a web of different colours, and I have to untangle and analyse them before I can work out why I'm feeling the way I am and how I can help myself.

I'll tell my mum I'm having an anxiety attack and

when she asks what's caused it, often I won't have a clue.

I could go from sitting happily one minute to feeling as though the world is caving in the next.

It's alarming for me, confusing, frightening and frustrating because I know there are people around me who want to help, but if I don't even know why I'm feeling that way, then how can they possibly know how to help me? As time has gone on, I've started to understand I have certain triggers which I am learning to identify.

The small talk most people have no problem engaging in has always been a huge problem for me, but I have learned to understand through listening and watching my mum.

When I walk the dog with her, she often stops and talks to people, and listening to her conversation helps me get used to 'chitchat' and get better at communicating myself. Still, some days I have episodes of shutdown where I would rather not have to speak at all. I don't know why it happens; I just know that I really can't talk. If anyone talks to me when I'm feeling like that, then I nod or answer with as few words as I can.

I pull up my hoodie because that makes me feel hidden and being hidden makes me feel safer and less anxious. I keep my head down so people can see I don't want to talk, and I hope no one talks to me.

If they do, I can't focus. I drift into my own world and often don't even hear what someone said.

In the supermarket once, a staff member stopped me and told me to put my hoodie down. I was with my mum, and I didn't mind because I was having a good day, but if I had been having a bad day, or I'd been on my own, the hoodie would have been my protective shell and being told to remove it would have meant me having to leave the store without buying what I needed.

When I was younger, I avoided making eye

contact with anyone other than my mum and brother; as I've gotten older, I've found this to be less difficult, but it can still be a problem with strangers.

I'm usually uncomfortable speaking on the telephone when other people are around, and I'm never sure what I'm supposed to say.

I can talk to my mum without any problems, but that's because I can't go wrong when I'm speaking to her. She understands the difficulties I have, so I don't feel self-conscious.

With other family members, or strangers, it's challenging for me to have a conversation on the phone, even now, and I avoid it unless I know who is calling; but I can also have 'good days' when I'm feeling particularly confident, and I can answer the phone and have a conversation without too much trouble. The odd thing about that is, although I feel a massive sense of achievement afterwards, I also often feel worried that I may have said the wrong thing or come across negatively.

One day I was expecting a call from the Open University, and although I was really nervous—in fact, I felt sick with nerves—I was surprised by how well I dealt with that conversation. I was being asked lots of questions about what I wanted to do and what interested me, and because I was able to talk about my interests, I managed the call well. The problems arise when I feel as though the conversation is happening too quickly, and I don't have enough time to process what I'm being asked or what I should say in reply.

I won't speak to call centres because I can't predict the questions I will be asked, and that unexpected aspect makes me feel anxious. The thought of it makes me avoid it altogether. I don't usually answer the phone to unknown numbers, and at times I just hang up. If I must make a call, I ask my mum to do it for me, and often she will answer my phone.

I don't enjoy what many kids my age find fun, and

I prefer to be by myself, doing my own thing. I have a lot of fun socialising online because I don't have the difficulties of face-to-face interaction and have time to think out my responses to people, which makes it a lot easier. I enjoy learning languages, and I interact with people online from different European countries because it helps me to be able to practice what I've learned by messaging them in their own language, but I choose to communicate via text messages online rather than voice chats, because I have more time to think of responses to questions and comments.

I had a bank account opened for me when I was eleven, so I could save money for things I needed; this was before my autism diagnosis, and a year ago I needed to speak to the bank because I had a problem with a payment I made online. My mum told me I should try to do it myself, so I called them while she was next to me offering support, but as soon as they asked me my date of birth I froze.

I know when I was born, it's a straightforward question, but because I was so scared of speaking to someone I didn't know and hadn't spoken to before, I didn't know what to expect and had an anxiety attack—my brain blanked out completely. The staff member on the other end of the phone said they didn't believe I was who I said I was and they could hear my mum speaking to me in the background, so they refused to help me after that, and since then I haven't attempted another phone call like that.

I have help when I write emails because I don't always know what to write, how to respond, or how to start a written conversation. Email for me is much better than talking on the phone or meeting in person, but it still has its downsides.

When my new computer was having problems, I messaged the company I bought it from, and they asked me to explain what was wrong with it. I struggled to put into words what I wanted to say. I also sometimes misread their question and ended up replying to what I thought the question was when I was being asked something completely different.

This happens to me a lot.

A conversation about a specific subject is easier for me than chitchat. If I'm walking the dog, and people pass by and say 'hi,' I can deal with it because I'm expecting it. Still, if they stop and go into a whole conversation, I feel awkward, like everything I say sounds weird and I've said something wrong, even though my family tells me I sound like an intelligent, fluent person. To me, inside my own head, nothing is coming out right.

In shops, until very recently, I would rather not go to the tills where people are serving. Instead, I usually used the self-serve checkouts because I didn't suffer the anxiety of having to talk to people. That could backfire when the machine stopped working and someone came up to help me, but thankfully this was rare.

Now I'm realising more and more that I do sound all right, I try to force myself into these situations so I can get used to having conversations with people. It's good to know that the discussion will be short-lived and as soon as my shopping is packed and paid for, the interaction is over.

A knock on the door usually causes me anxiety, especially if it's unexpected. So many questions race through my mind. Will I be expected to talk, and how long will they keep me at the door? Will I have to invite them in? How will I know if I'm acting the right way? Recently, on good days, I can deal with this, which is encouraging for me because there was a time when I wondered if I would ever feel able to cope with it. The problems come when I'm not having a good day. For example, faith groups or salespeople knock more than once or stand there for a long time waiting for me to open the door because it looks like there's someone home. They feel they have the right to stand at the door knocking for what seems like ages and it makes me feel vulnerable and unsafe, like my privacy is invaded. I just want them to leave my front door.

Another cause of anxiety is a missed delivery card posted through the front door, when they've left a parcel with a neighbour I don't know. That forces me to interact with a stranger, and if I don't knock on their door, then I don't know when they will come and knock on mine. Either way, I'm forced into a situation I may not feel able to deal with at the time.

I don't like getting a letter because I wonder if I will have to make a phone call. My mum deals with my finances and any communication relating to me, so while I'm young, it's not such a problem. I hope that in a few years I will feel more comfortable taking over my own responsibilities, but right now I can't deal with the anxiety all these situations cause, and I end up either shutting down or spiraling into a meltdown.

It would help if call centres, post workers,

businesses and charities were more autism aware. So often we have to make phone calls or people call us expecting us to answer, but autism makes this really difficult. An email is so much more autism friendly and far less intrusive from strangers.

I'm worried about how I will cope as I get older with form filling and starting my own business. I've looked into several possible jobs I could do, which would mean I would be able to work predominantly alone. Still, there's no getting away from the fact I have to learn how to deal with communication for every aspect of my life, from finances, to getting a home one day, and dealing with customers. I know I have a long way to go, but I also know I am determined to learn more coping skills as I get older and have more confidence in myself. I know I can do anything I put my mind to once I learn how to deal with these situations, and I'm working on it.

What has helped me!

- ✓ Putting an autism sign on the front door.
- ✓ Using self-serve tills.
- ✓ Asking my mum to deal with communication on my behalf.
- ✓ Asking family to prepare me before anyone is invited into the house.
- ✓ Setting goals and pushing myself out of my comfort zone to help give me more confidence.
- ✓ Realising I might feel like I'm getting it all wrong, but most of the time other people don't notice and think I'm doing fine.

Communication Notes

Write what helps you!

TRAVEL

When I was very little, I didn't mind travelling on the bus because I always sat next to the window and used to enjoy watching the world go by. I didn't have to speak to anyone I didn't know—in fact, I was discouraged from speaking to strangers—and if there were any conversations to be had, my mother would always be the one chatting.

I haven't tried to get on a bus by myself, because I really hate the idea of having to deal with anything unexpected while traveling alone. There are too many potential problems that could go wrong for me.

I'd have to speak to the bus driver, and what if I wasn't sure which stop I needed to get off at?

Would I have to talk to other people on the bus— would they start a conversation with me when I'm not ready for one?

Would they be offended or upset if I went into shutdown and didn't want to speak to them when they talked to me? Would that be considered rude?

If someone sat next to me and their perfume or aftershave was too strong, that would be difficult, and I'd be stuck because I wouldn't want to have to speak to ask to move past them. I would worry that I might offend them by moving to another seat, so I would have to suffer until it was time to get off the bus or leave before my stop so I could get out of the situation.

Sometimes contemplating journeys with a lot of

people around me that I don't know makes me panic, which is why I have never attempted to get on a bus or train alone. I know I will have more confidence as time goes on and I get older, and I know I'm lucky I have support around me, so I don't have to put myself in these situations before I'm ready.

I hate not being in control and having to rely on someone else to get me somewhere. The other problem on public transport is the level of noise and the large crowds which often gather at rush hour.

I have the same concerns about the train. As a child, I loved to travel on trains because when you're little, there's no pressure on you to talk to people and we only travelled during times when it was quiet.

The process of buying a ticket isn't as bad, I suppose, and you can buy them online now because there are automatic ticket machines. But once I'm on the train, I would be nervously waiting for the ticket person to come up and speak to me. I hate having to communicate with strangers, no matter how nice or professional they are. It isn't that I can't do it, because sometimes I can; it's the anxiety of knowing there's no choice if I feel like I can't.

My heart would race because I would somehow convince myself I'd got on the wrong train, or something wasn't right.

I tend to make the worst-case scenarios up in my mind in preparation for the worst thing to happen. I want to think of every possible outcome so I can prepare myself—whatever that may be, that way it won't be a surprise and I feel in control of the situation. But even if I knew I had a fully paid ticket, if a ticket collector started asking me questions, I would panic. I don't want to be put on the spot. People around would stare at me, and I would have no idea what to do. I would end up shutting down or melting down and would convince myself I had the wrong ticket, and what if I did have the wrong ticket, would they throw me off the train, or accuse me of fare-dodging and call the police?

My special interest has been cars since I was two years old. As a child, I always loved the sensory experience of being driven and fell asleep almost as soon as we set off for long journeys.

When I can drive myself, I'll be in control and can enjoy more independence.

I feel confident on the road and have been taking young driver lessons since I was fourteen, when my mum bought an hour lesson for me for a Christmas present. It seems to be taking forever to get to seventeen now, even though I'm only a few months away. I'm so happy I'll soon be able to drive—I'm literally ticking off the days.

I've always loved cycling; when I was little, I went on bike rides with my dad and brother in a large group. We'd cycle for a few miles in the countryside. I didn't mind being in a group then because it made me feel invisible, and no one talks to you while you're cycling.

I had no interest in riding a motorbike though, I'd always thought they were dangerous—at least more dangerous than a car, but my mum encouraged me to take my CBT (compulsory basic training) because she wanted me to have some independence and said it would give me confidence. I couldn't do the test with a stranger by myself, so she booked herself on a CBT course along with me so I wouldn't have to do it alone. I'm glad she did because I wasn't prepared to go out on the road test by myself when the time came, so it was good she was there.

I started to feel panicked and didn't want to carry on after a few minutes on the road, but I forced myself to do it because I knew that when I passed, I would have more independence. It has improved my confidence such a lot; I love riding my bike. I'm able to get around now, and I'm fine filling my bike with petrol at the self-serve pumps, whereas before I never left the house alone.

I am getting more confident by the day and force myself to step out of my comfort zone on my better days.

Motorbiking has had its downsides, though. With a small bike engine, I can barely keep up with traffic, and I feel vulnerable not being able to get up to the national speed limit.

Where I live there are a lot of country lanes with steep hills and if I have a lot of cars queuing behind me, I feel exposed because I know I'm holding other people up, which causes me anxiety and makes me overthink. I avoid busy roads, rush hour and use back streets whenever I can so I don't have to worry so much about holding people up when they're trying to get to work or home.

I wouldn't want to have to ride or drive somewhere far where I would need to stay overnight. I don't like staying somewhere that isn't my home because I don't feel comfortable. I need to have my bed, my things and my own space.

Overnight stays in hotels or my family's houses are too different, and I never feel safe.

When I have stayed overnight, I just wish I was back home. When I was a child, even when I was on holiday, I asked my mum how many days we had left before we went home and always looked forward to it.

When I've had to stay at my family's houses, I feel anxious; although I've always tried really hard not to show it or upset people, I never enjoy it. Now we are planning to visit family for a birthday and, even though it's a month away, I feel nervous every time I think about it. I wish I could drive right now because I'd be able to drive myself there and back in a day.

As a child, being stuck in traffic used to terrify me. I had severe panic attacks until we could go, because I had no way of predicting how long we were going to be stuck on the road, not moving. I was literally stuck in my anxiety, which would end up with me having a meltdown. I hate the idea of being stuck somewhere, because I need to be in control.

I wouldn't attempt to go on a plane on my own—it literally seems like hell.

When I'm older, it might not be so bad, but if you ask me now about the worst public transport, I would have to go on by myself, my answer would be a plane.

Airports are hellish, because of how crowded and noisy they are. I have the same problems as with any other public transport, but its compounded by the size of the airport and the stress of knowing I'm going so far away from my comfort zone.

With family, when I go on a plane, it's easier because I can cocoon myself in the window seat, put on my headphones and watch films, knowing I don't have to talk to anyone.

My mum will take care of the tickets and everything for me.

Long queues are a nightmare for me, and that isn't just in airports, that's anywhere. Generally, I don't like lines and if I don't have to stand in one, then I won't.

When I think about other people coping with all these things I struggle with, I don't know how they do it. I feel jealous; I wish I felt safe talking to other people and had the level of independence many other kids my age enjoy.

Even at sixteen, I still don't feel comfortable attempting to get on a bus or train because of these issues, and I cope with staying overnight with family by reminding myself that it won't be long until I'm back home.

Driving a car will help a lot because it will give

me so much confidence. I'll be able to put my dog in the car and take him for a walk at our local nature reserve, go shopping and put the bags in the boot instead of being limited to how much I can carry on my bike, and I'll be able to visit family a few hours away, who often need help, knowing I can get home the same day.

What has helped me!

- ✓ I have a disability photo card which I can show people if I'm alone and find it challenging to communicate.
- ✓ Making sure people I travel with understand that I may have difficulties in some situations.
- ✓ Avoiding rush hour or busy times where the level of noise, traffic or people will be greater.
- ✓ Bringing my own bedding and music with me when I stay away from home.

Travel Notes
Write what helps you!

SOCIALISATION

For me there are different forms of socialisation. There are the interactions I have with people I've known for a long time, and then the interactions I have with friends online and people I meet day to day when going to the shops or walking the dog.

They are very different, and I deal with varying degrees of anxiety in each case.

When I was six to ten years old, I was fortunate enough to be in a lot of social groups with my mum and brother, which were based on specific activities or interests. For example, meeting up at the beach to study natural history or to go for a swim and going on woodland walks, or survival days, learning how to find food in the wood, cook it and make a den using sticks and leaves. I was with a lot of kids, but they were different ages and had different abilities and needs.

Socialising wasn't stressful because there were no expectations of me to play with the other kids. We were all in the same place, and we could interact, or not, but there was no pressure, and we all stayed for as long as we wanted and left when we'd had enough. I would often spend a week at home after socializing all day to get the energy up again for the next week. As a child, I took part regularly in these groups, but each time was a little different. There were different groups of kids every time, so we knew each other, but we were never in the exact same group because not everyone always joined us. We were all different ages, so sometimes we'd do things that were more for the little ones, and other times it was more for the older siblings. I enjoyed those groups, I enjoyed helping the younger kids and also liked being one of the oldest there because I liked taking on responsibilities.

As I've grown up, I've preferred not to go to social groups anymore because I'm so much happier doing my own thing. Now I get more enjoyment from speaking to my mum's friends than kids my age because the conversations seem so much more interesting.

In group situations where age is the only basis for me to be put with other people, for example in an after-school drama class, I found it impossible to interact, because I had nothing in common with them. When we were asked to form a group, I stood around waiting for the groups to form until the teacher came and told me which group to go into and then I'd usually just stand watching, waiting for them to decide what we were doing. I'd ask them to tell me what they wanted me to do and then I'd just do it.

When I walk the dog, people come up to me and want to talk about the dogs; this is something I struggle with, especially when I'm having one of my 'shutdown mornings,' as I call them. This is when I don't speak for a few hours in the morning, which is common for me. I usually need a couple of hours to prepare myself for the day, so if anyone tries to talk to me, I'll just nod as my answer.

If I'm shopping in town, I'll prepare myself beforehand. I expect people in shops to talk to me, especially where I live because people are generally very friendly and kind. It's not so bad when it happens, and I'm expecting it, as long as the conversation isn't prolonged.

In the supermarket I won't ask if I need help finding something. If I can't find it myself, I'll leave without it. I know that it seems like such a basic skill, to ask a staff member a simple question, but for me, it's a minefield of social expectations which I'm not always prepared for.

When I do spend time with other people, they're people who share similar interests, so there's always something to talk about. My brother often asks me to speak with his friends online and join them with him in games, but I can't bring myself to do it. I can talk to the friends I've made about the interests we share, but it's completely different when I'm asked to interact with someone new because I have no idea what to expect from them.

Emotionally I feel a lot younger than my age, but intellectually I feel much older.

I don't understand ulterior motives. If I want or need something, I will ask, but I know in the past people have expected me to understand their request or need simply by implying it.

Indirect communication confuses me. I prefer people to be emotionally honest about what they want or need because I'm usually happy to do what I can, but sometimes it feels as though I'm expected to be psychic.

Some people have accused me of not caring, or

not listening, or perhaps being deliberately rude or unkind because I've nodded but not elaborated after their efforts to communicate, but that's not the case.

This makes me feel annoyed and frustrated because people don't seem to realise they're asking me to use the same skills I'm struggling with to explain why I'm struggling with them.

Often it makes me feel like it's not worth trying at all. I may as well not bother to try if I'm going to be criticised anyway when I do.

Socialising in my teens has been so different from when I was younger. I'm home educated, so the kids I socialised with growing up were mostly home educated too, and we were always out and about, never sitting down still anywhere. In those groups, there was always a lot of support and help to learn how to socialise and co-operate with each other, and because of that, those groups were so much easier because we all had an element of control and we weren't forced into situations with other people. Now the idea of being in a group or class full of kids my own age, with perhaps only one adult to mentor us, worries me.

I don't like being in a class because I feel as though I'm being watched. I'm never confident in what I'm doing and always feel as though my awkwardness is drawing unwanted attention from other people.

I need to be free to move around and remove myself from my environment if I'm sensing a difficult vibe.

When I was little one of the groups my mum put me into was a rugby class, because my friend enjoyed rugby and he convinced me to give it a try. For weeks I'd go to the matches and stand in the middle of the field, not having a clue what I was supposed to be doing.

One day I watched the rugby ball fly towards me, and I felt sure it couldn't hit me because the pitch was huge, but I was wrong, it hit me in the face!

I decided rugby wasn't for me.

Luckily, when I told my mum I didn't enjoy playing, she stopped taking me. We tried other hobbies instead, but every time I was in groups with other kids I tended to follow along, struggling to communicate, even when I had something I wanted to say. I find it impossible within a group setting to express myself or my needs.

Birthday parties as a kid were sometimes okay, but it depended on whether there was a lot of adult interaction. As long as I knew where I was supposed to be and what I was supposed to be doing, I was okay, but left to my own devices with a lot of kids I didn't have anything in common with, I just stood there, lost, never knowing what to do or think. I tended to shut down, because I don't know how to express myself when I feel lost, even now. The forced association in a lot of group situations doesn't feel like socialisation to me; it feels like a serious punishment.

A huge challenge is when I'm with someone, and they bump into a friend of theirs who I don't know. To me, they're a stranger, so I might not feel comfortable talking to them. I tend to go into shutdown while I'm busy internally processing the situation, which I know sometimes looks rude or unfriendly.

What has helped me!

- ✓ Not being forced to socialise when I'm not feeling comfortable, or I'm already anxious.
- ✓ Joining clubs with friends or my brother for support and having adults nearby to help when I've fallen out of my depth.
- ✓ Accepting my difficulties aren't my fault and that no matter how much I might want to, I can't pretend to be like everyone else when I'm not.

Socialisation Notes

Write what helps you!

FOCUS

My concentration has two settings; hyper-focused and unfocused.

 It takes me a good ten minutes to get into a mindset where my attention is focused on an activity, but once I am, I'm absorbed in it, and I can continue for hours.

Any interruptions infuriate me when I'm hyper-focused because it takes me so long to concentrate again afterwards.

 I struggle to plan my day, but somehow it always seems to go wrong. As soon as a minor detail changes I'm completely thrown off, and it feels like my whole day is ruined.

When I organise myself, I tend to micromanage everything. I like plans to be arranged down to the last minute. I can stay focused on something for hours—like my work, designing, and writing, but as soon as my focus is interrupted, my concentration fails me. When I'm riding my motorbike, I'm at my most focused because I'm aware of the dangers. I know some people won't even see me on the road, and I have to account for that. I look out for every possible hazard and assume I'm invisible to the rest of the traffic.

When I was little, I couldn't switch focus, but now it's not so hard as long as it's something I'm interested in, although it still takes a few minutes for me to adjust to the switch.

Organizational skills and motivation are something I have problems regulating. I'm either doing really well, and everything is going perfectly, or it's not working at all.

If my focus gets drawn away from what I'm doing, for example, running a bath, it's not unlike me to completely forget that I'm doing it, and I end up flooding the bathroom floor.

I've had a few incidents with the oven, forgetting I've put it on and going downstairs a few hours later and realising I was going to make something to eat. I've managed to set the stove on fire because I had a plastic bag next to the hob and didn't realise it caught fire.

I also managed to set fire to baking paper inside the oven when I was making cookies one day. I'm fortunate that my house still stands vertically!

Focus is something I have to consider when I'm doing anything. It's difficult for me when I am focused, especially during a conversation, because I have to be able to finish what I wanted to say before anyone interrupts me.

I freeze if I'm not allowed to finish what I was saying and struggle to cut myself off and change my thought process quickly.

Almost all my motivation outside of my special interests is sparked by other people, and it's difficult for me to organise my daily routine unless it's repetitive and becomes a habit.

Even just remembering to eat is an issue for me. I have two settings; not hungry and starving. When I don't eat enough, I feel a little nauseous, which my mum keeps telling me means I'm hungry, and I need to have something in my stomach. Other times I overeat and feel sick because I think I'm still hungry and keep eating.

I enjoy eating healthy food, though, and enjoy salads and vegetables every day, but I do need reminding to make sure I'm getting enough calories and drinking enough water, especially when I'm hyper-focused on something and don't want to take a break.

My mum reminds me to eat and nags me to keep a bowl of nuts at my desk, so I keep my energy levels up.

I often find my mind wanders. If I'm in the middle of a thought and someone asks me a question or asks me to do something, I will respond physically with an automatic nod, but I haven't actually heard the question, or it hasn't sunk into my long-term memory, so I forget. I can often get in trouble with friends or family later on because they've expected me to do something or have assumed I've agreed to something, which later on I will argue that I am a hundred per cent sure they didn't mention to me.

This can cause a lot of problems for me; the slightest distraction which causes my mind to wander can throw me off completely. Sensory difficulties are an issue here, too, so I've mentioned those in the sensory challenges chapter.

What has helped me!

- ✓ Staying away from environments with too

many distractions.

- ✓ If I can't have total silence, then I find listening to music with headphones on helpful when I'm studying. The music drowns out other background distractions and helps me focus on what I'm doing.
- ✓ Healthy snacks—I like to have a bowl of nuts to snack on for energy, and a large bottle of water.
- ✓ Making sure I'm not too hot or too cold, because sensory issues can make focusing impossible.
- ✓ Asking people to have patience with me, as I need to finish talking before I can change the subject.
- ✓ Making sure friends and family understand that I need to be one hundred per cent focused on them if they want to ask me a question and be sure I've actually heard them.

Focus Notes
Write what helps you!

ANXIETY

I have learned that certain triggers cause anxiety for me, and the running theme is being out of control.

My comfort zone is my home and the area where I live. I always feel out of my comfort zone when I'm told I have to go somewhere I've never been before because I feel a lack of control, even when I'm with family.

Standstill traffic is a trigger for me because there's no indication of how long we will be stuck there. If I'm moving with the traffic, however slowly, I feel okay—I know eventually I'll get to the next junction.

I don't have a panic attack in the way I used to when I was younger, but my anxiety levels are through the roof until the traffic starts to move.

When I was a child, I couldn't go in lifts because I was afraid that there would be a mechanical malfunction and we would be stuck. As I've grown, I realise it's unlikely to happen, and I don't feel so nervous about it.

 Another trigger is overthinking. Since I can remember, I've put a lot of pressure on myself to be responsible. I take on responsibilities even when they're not mine because I feel I need to take control. I worry about our animals all the time. Even when they're fine, I think about possible problems—like, if I haven't cleaned out the guinea pigs' cage properly, even though I know I have. If we're in traffic and the dog is in the car, what happens if we're there too long and he gets thirsty, and we can't get him any water?

Unexpected situations and sensory difficulties are also huge triggers for my anxiety.

I get physical signs of anxiety quite quickly. Usually, when I don't know what the problem is, my heart starts to beat really fast, then I start to feel sick, and I often shake fiercely. If I don't pinpoint the trigger for my anxiety in time, it will lead to a complete shutdown or meltdown.

The best way I have learned to cope with it is to sit down and take deep breaths and think through the reasons why I feel triggered. I mustn't let myself get overwhelmed because then I lose the ability to regain control. Recently I started learning cognitive behavioural therapy online, which has helped too. I enjoy practicing mindfulness and taking our dog for a walk always puts me in a good frame of mind.

As I've gotten older, I haven't relied so much on my mum when I feel panicked and can deal with it better on my own, but as a young child I confided in my mum when I was anxious. She would run me a bath with my favourite scents and talk me through the process, reassuring me that the anxiety would pass and helping me take my mind off it. Even if it was the middle of the night, sometimes we'd get a game out or watch a film together.

Now that I'm so much older, I deal with it a lot better because I tell myself it's just autism and that I can take control if I take deep breaths and try to calm myself down.

Growing up, I would never admit to feeling anxious with anyone other than my mum because I knew they wouldn't understand. There were times when I was accused of spoiling the day for other people because I'd had a bad panic attack and needed to remove myself from a situation, which made everything much worse. But once I was diagnosed, some of those people started to realise that it's not something I can control, and it became more accepted with extended family.

When it came time to take my CBT, I know my

instructor didn't notice my panic halfway through the road ride, but my mum did, so she talked me through it.

Even a small change in the house can make me feel uneasy. For example, re-organising a room.

Clutter is also a big problem for me. I need to have a place for things and for them to remain in their place. If my environment is a mess, so is my mind, but that doesn't mean I'm good at organizing – far from it! I'll let things get messy up to a point and then I'll have to have a thorough tidy up.

Often just tidying up my bedroom can put me into a whole new mood. I feel calmer if my surroundings are clear of clutter. A change can be for the better, but if I'm not expecting it, then it can still cause me distress because anything that slightly alters in my environment puts me on edge if it's a shock.

I buy the same clothes when I find something I

like. I recently found jeans which were super comfortable and went back to buy three more pairs in the same colour. Clothes must be comfortable, otherwise they are a sensory distraction which makes me irritated and annoyed. For example, I'm bothered if the inside of a coat is too warm, fuzzy, too scratchy or jumpers aren't soft enough or shirts are too scratchy. But what is most distressing for me is that often I have no idea what has caused me to fall into a panic, and the stress overwhelms me for no apparent reason. This is a nightmare!

When I'm in an intense panic, I feel like I'm going to be sick, then I get dizzy and have a headache, and often feel either really hot or really cold. When this happens, I have a warm bath, then I often want to sit in complete silence and try to sleep. Herbal tea often helps, and talking to my mum about it, if I need to process something. She understands how I feel, so often she can take my mind off it long enough for the panic to ease, and then I can fall asleep.

I don't look as though I have a disability, and on a good day when I do communicate, I'm told I do it well enough for people not to realise the sheer terror and panic which races through me when I complete the simplest social interactions that I'm not prepared for.

What has helped me!

- ✓ Explaining to family and friends how anxiety affects me.
- ✓ Having my feelings validated and not being made to feel guilty for having to stop an activity.
- ✓ Removing myself from the situation if I feel myself becoming anxious and finding somewhere quiet where I can calm down.

Anxiety Notes
Write what helps you!

SOOTHING BEHAVIOURS - STIMMING

I have a few different soothing behaviours. I pace, I click my fingers, tap my foot, rub the nails on my right hand against those on my left hand and repeat noises at times too, or talk to myself. Usually, when I'm nervous, I pace.

The repetitive action of walking up and down soothes me and helps me think. When I'm sitting, I tap my foot a lot which can be attributed to any emotion—it's a soothing action which allows me to concentrate and focus. Often sitting at the table, I would kick the chair leg or breakfast bar, which frequently upset the adults around me. As a young child, I used to flap my hands a lot when I was excited.

When I've psyched myself up to speak on the phone, I pace up and down or walk in circles; it helps me concentrate and focus on the conversation. I would often jump from sofa to sofa when I was little or spin in circles.

Stimming doesn't bother me. I don't notice it, but people around me do which isn't a problem for me. It would become a problem if I were told to stop because it would break my concentration or put the focus on me, which I would want to avoid at all costs. I always want to flee a situation when I am made the focus of attention.

I prefer to feel invisible most of the time, or at least not feel responsible for maintaining a conversation with anyone. I need to stim to process and stay calm, so if I were told to stop, I would shut down and then attempt to remove myself from the environment as quickly as possible.

When I'm concentrating, I don't notice that I'm stimming; even if I do stop, I usually start again not long afterwards, and I never realise I'm doing it until someone else points it out. For me stimming is a crucial part of concentrating. I'm easily distracted, and it can take me a lot of time to get into a pattern of focus, so if I'm snapped out of that, it takes a while for me to get back into a focused mindset.

What has helped me!

✓ Making family and friends aware that I'm not being deliberately disruptive when I stim. Not only is it a genuine need, but it can also alert them to a potential meltdown. When I was at my college interview, waiting to be seen, it was my stimming that let my mum know I was headed for a meltdown.

Soothing Behaviour Notes
Write what helps you!

EMPATHY /ACCEPTING GIFTS

When I was nine and started the drama classes, I can remember in one lesson we were told to put on white masks and to use only body language to show a specific emotion. This was the first time I had ever experienced movement or expression as a way to figure out how people were feeling. It was a lightbulb moment which was really helpful for me to learn.

There are times when I can tell if someone is feeling upset, but if I don't pick it up, unless you tell me, I won't know.

I recently watched a former FBI agent talk about

how he looked at people's actions and their posture to find out things about them, things that they were subconsciously hiding. When I watch things like that, it makes me realise how much I miss, but even people who aren't on the spectrum overlook the more subtle forms of body language. The difference is, I miss a bit more.

If someone tells me they feel sad, worried, confused, upset or happy, then I will share in that emotion with them and do what I can to help or celebrate, depending on what's needed.

People in the past have assumed I understood how someone was feeling and got upset when I didn't respond with enough empathy.

It isn't empathetic for a non-autistic person to judge an autistic person as if they had abilities they don't have; so, in that case, it seems it isn't only autistic people who need to consider whether they are showing enough empathy. I have a lot of empathy and sympathy; what I don't have, is the decoding programme in my brain to work out what someone is feeling or needs, without being told.

I can feel the vibe in a place, which often confuses me. For example, if people are quiet and the mood is sad, but no one will admit to being unhappy, then I want to leave, because for me to feel comfortable in an environment, the mood and the vibe have to match. Otherwise, I sense I'm being lied to; perhaps to other people, there may be a lot of body language or facial expressions which tell the other people in the room why they are sad, and they think it's obvious, but I may not have understood what is happening and that makes me feel on edge.

I may come across to others as being quite reserved, uncaring and prickly if they attempt to make conversation with me when I'm feeling this way.

I've heard other autistic people mention this too. It's almost as though by not having the ability to understand facial expressions, body language and tone of emotion, we make up for it with a sixth sense almost, and pick up the energy in the room instead.

When I give gifts to people, I need to know what they want. I want to be given specific requests so that I know what to buy them.

If I'm asked to surprise someone with a gift, I usually don't have any idea what to buy. I love giving things to people and if someone says they don't want anything, I now realise what they really mean is that they want something nice, but they want me to figure out what that nice thing is without any help. I don't like that—it's stressful, and, I think, unnecessary. I send flowers to women and buy gift cards for men now.

The most challenging part of gift giving is worrying about not having the right reaction or facial expression when I open a present from someone else.

As a young child, I was often accused of not being

grateful enough for gifts by some family members, which upset me because I don't know how to prove when I'm thankful. I take gifts and say thank you, but I don't make a big deal of it, even when I'm given presents that I absolutely love.

I'm told I don't show happiness no matter how happy I feel inside.

I would prefer it if I was given a wrapped gift and didn't have to open it in front of anyone, and then was able to say thank you later on when I could process and articulate the response I want to give.

As a child, I used to hate accepting gifts on my birthday because I had to pretend to like them even if I didn't, which I found hard because I was always told not to lie. I assumed if I was asked a question they wanted a truthful answer, otherwise, why ask the question? Now I know asking a question just to get a specific answer is common, but sometimes, I go into default and answer without thinking. Still, I really don't ever want to hurt anyone's feelings.

What has helped me!

- ✓ Learning more about body language and facial expressions. I don't always get it right, but I've learned to be proud of myself for doing my best.
- ✓ Learning the difference between lies and white lies which save people's feelings— and when to use them.
- ✓ My family learning that just because I haven't shown emotion when I've received a gift, it doesn't mean I'm not grateful.
- ✓ Asking family to let me open a gift in private without any pressure.
- ✓ Asking for help when I need to buy gifts for other people.
- ✓ Accepting my feelings and not being made to feel bad if I need to leave a situation when I'm uncomfortable.

Empathy / Accepting Gifts

Write what helps you!

EDUCATION

As a child, my mum bought me a whole load of phonics books, but they didn't work for me as I couldn't blend the sounds together. I learned to read by learning each word separately by sight. I learn the same way I see the world, which is visual; I need the whole picture to remember it. As soon as my mum bought a sight-reading program, I was reading almost straight away at the age of four. Interestingly, my little brother, who also couldn't learn with phonics, didn't learn to read until he was ten, and yet he's really good at English now and loves to read.

When I'm looking at a page full of writing, I can see the tracks through the text where the spaces are between the words. Like snakes sliding down the page or pictures.

If I'm not interested in the subject, it's tough for me to feel motivated or concentrate because my mind wanders, and I start to focus on things which do interest me.

During those times, if I'm being spoken to, I rarely hear what is being said, and if I'm reading the text, I don't understand what I'm reading. I can end up re-reading the same sentence over and over and still have no clue what I just read.

I enjoy learning languages; I've tried many ways to learn, and the best one for me is to watch YouTube videos of native speakers with the words shown on the screen and building on sentences which I can then go and use in everyday life to remember them.

Workbooks displaying grammar and colours and

numbers aren't interesting to me. I prefer to learn to speak foreign languages within the context of whole sentences.

I can't write fast, I'm left-handed, and writing has always been difficult for me, so I avoid it. I have studied my GCSEs online, but I chose not to take the exams because I feel anxious, and my mind goes blank. I can't write the answers down in time, I often don't understand the questions, and I wouldn't have the confidence to raise my hand and ask a stranger to help me. I want to gain qualifications, but I get angry when I feel confused by the questions or get a wrong mark because I have the right answer but haven't written it the way I was supposed to. My brain works fast, especially in math's and to having to slow it down to write every thought process when working out a sum, puts me in a muddle and I get infuriated. At the vet recently she got out a calculator to work out our fee; I had worked it out immediately in my head, and the annoying thing is, she probably has a brilliant math's grade!

When studying English, questions like 'what do you notice about the language used in this text?' confused me, because my answer was that they are speaking English.

When I tried to study using curriculum workbooks, often the lessons weren't clear to me. There wasn't enough detail, and my mum had to explain what I assume a lot of kids would have already understood from the question, but I didn't. I need precise questions with no room for interpretation.

A guided answer would work better for me in the later stage of education as well as in the younger versions, especially for English, because I often worked out the question from the possible answers. Multiple choice questions would help because I'd gradually learn the type of answers that they were looking for. So, when the question asked, 'what do you notice about the language used?' if there had been a multiple-choice answer, then I would have understood the question by seeing the options. I think this would have helped me learn the 'language' of the questions and how to interpret their meaning.

Math's is enjoyable for me, but what I did find really hard, though, was when the subject changed quickly, and I didn't have enough time to process that change.

I chose to study in days rather than time slots, so each day would be a specific subject, and I could get hyper-focused on that subject for as long as I needed to until I understood it.

I've enjoyed studying courses which interest me online as well. I've completed a car maintenance course, and more recently the cognitive behavioural therapy course, and I like learning about nutrition through scientific sites like nutritionfacts.org, as well as having fun learning sentences in Spanish, Mandarin, French and Swedish.

When I was in primary level, my mum used my

special interests to teach me lots of different subjects.

I remember we had toy cars lined up when I started learning maths. She'd tell me to park a certain number of vehicles (in a huge toy multi-storey car park I had with a petrol pump at the bottom), and she'd teach me addition and subtraction by moving the cars in front of me. There were also a lot of games and puzzles my mum bought from Orchard Toys, which were really helpful—the bus stop game was fun. I remember we played that a lot.

My brother was crazy about dinosaurs, so we'd look up on a map where bones have been found and talk about natural history.

I love going to museums and taking day trips to exciting places when there aren't any crowds.

I haven't found learning easy; most of the time my mum had to change the way she was interpreting a question for me several times before I finally got it, and there were times she had to leave a subject altogether and come back to it months or even years later before it actually made sense to me. But once it does, I'm good at remembering what I learn.

As I've grown, English has become harder for me. The earlier lessons, going through grammar rules, spelling, punctuation, and learning how to structure sentences, nouns, adjectives and pronouns, etc...were easier for me than having to give my opinion on a text. That confuses me because I rarely have an opinion, and I don't know how to think one up to answer the question. I still don't understand the point of most of the questions I was asked in the English tests and as exams aren't available in a format I understand, or an environment I'm able to concentrate in, I'm locked out of opportunities. The general belief is that without certain exam results, you're stupid, and yet so many of my friends say they couldn't complete the same grade in their exam now, because they only remembered it long enough to complete the exams. What is the point of that? It would be helpful for autistic people if we were assessed on our own capabilities, instead of only having one system for everyone. It's difficult to feel motivated when I'm fighting against a system which feels as though it's set up to fail me before I've even started.

I enjoy learning how to put things together, and I can put up cabinets and shelves. I learned to use a drill when I was younger and am interested in things like fire safety, first aid and cognitive behavioural therapy, which I think are all useful skills.

I'd like to work in a trade, and I like the idea of being self-employed because I need to be in control, so being my own boss and being able to work for myself is ideal. I'm not afraid of working hard because I like having something to do, and I get a sense of achievement when I complete tasks.

What has helped me!

- ✓ Being able to study at my own pace.
- ✓ Finding a learning environment which is free of distraction and using headphones if I need to block out external noise.
- ✓ Asking for things to be explained several different ways until I understand.
- ✓ Leaving topics which are too tricky and coming back to them at a later date.
- ✓ Learning that I don't have to compare myself to other people. I should judge myself on my capabilities and how much I'm improving day by day, not by how other kids my age are doing.

Education Notes

Write what helps you!

MELTDOWNS /SHUTDOWNS

Meltdowns, for me, happen when I'm not coping, and I display sudden and unexpected emotional distress. This can manifest as crying, shaking, being sick and removing myself immediately from a situation.

Shutdowns are more subtle. I'm not coping, so I go mute and cannot involve myself with people. When attacks happen, I could be anywhere. One of my most intense meltdowns was when I was at a firework display where there was loud music, lots of people and thunderous bangs.

I hated it. It started to rain, I was cold, and I lost control. I felt scared and wanted to leave, but my dad didn't know I had autism then and thought I was just complaining because it was cold.

It was just too loud, and a terrifying moment for me. I remember falling to the ground, my vision blurred, all I could hear was the sound of my heart beating, and everything went into slow motion.

I ended up shutting down and dragging my dad to the entrance, trying to tell him I wanted to go back to my grandparents' house. I felt sick afterwards, and it took hours for me to calm down.

The best way for me to deal with attacks is to find somewhere quiet where I can calm down as soon as possible, away from prying eyes.

It doesn't help when people don't understand the severity of the emotion behind the attack. It may not always show. It's a catch-22 because I don't like drawing attention to myself, so losing control is torturous on so many levels. I don't want to be made to feel bad, I can't feel worse than I already do and when it happens to me, it's often a reaction to too many stimuli which I can't control.

When I was thirteen, my mum bought my brother a golden retriever puppy—this was the event which led to my diagnosis of autism. We had been to meet the puppy and brought it home a few days later. He was a dog for my little brother and his extreme anxiety attacks. My brother's difficulties were always more apparent than mine because he used to explode regularly when he wasn't coping, but he didn't seem to have a problem with the puppy's high-pitched bark that hurt my ears.

I hadn't expected that. I also hadn't expected his teeth to be so sharp or for him to try to playfully chew on my leg or arm at every opportunity.

We had a German shepherd when I was younger,

but I remembered her in the later stages of her life when she was calm and tranquil, so this crazy little puppy sent me into an unexpected, emotional spin.

He always wanted to play and was bouncing around continuously.

Now that puppy is a massive part of our lives. When I feel sad, I cuddle our dog, and I immediately feel better.

As time has gone on, I have learnt to prepare for a possible meltdown or shutdown in advance. I feel like I get gut feelings and often if I'm not feeling confident enough, I can't leave home.

My meltdown triggers are too much sensory information at once and being forced into a social situation I can't control.

Unexpected situations are a worse trigger for me. Busy places with a lot of sounds are impossible for me to remain calm in. Fairgrounds, firework displays, the cinema and busy shops are all likely to throw me into a meltdown if I don't properly prepare.

Now that I'm older, I can see more clearly when I'm starting to lose control, and I take myself out of the situation as soon as I can.

As long as I'm in control of my environment, I can do that. I don't use public transport or go anywhere where there will be large crowds because I need to be able to leave a situation I'm not coping with. Since I've had my bike, it's been so much easier because I feel more confident just knowing I have more control in my environment, and I can go for a short ride and clear my head if I need to.

What has helped me!

- ✓ Learning my triggers to help to avoid a crisis.
- ✓ Moving into a safe space.
- ✓ Asking for support when I need it.

Meltdowns/Shutdowns Notes

Write what helps you!

OVERTHINKING

My overthinking is often triggered by social interaction and anxiety.

I recently went to a grocery store, and outside at the side of the road there was a police car. My thoughts strayed to reasons I might be stopped, and I started ticking off a list in my mind. Is my helmet strapped on properly? Are my lights working? Has my L plate fallen off and I haven't noticed? Could there be an error in a computer entry, if they check I have insurance would it come up that I don't?

I panic about panicking; it's a vicious cycle.

If a police officer actually did pull me over, I'd probably look so guilty from the sheer panic on my face, they'd be sure there was something they should be charging me with.

I have a disabled card with me which makes me feel a bit better, because I know I can show that first to explain why I may not act or react the way people might expect in some situations. As I know I don't look like I have a disability, that card is my safety net, and without it, people would be forgiven for thinking there's absolutely nothing different about my brain compared to theirs.

I overthink because I'm trying to prepare myself for every perceivable outcome, so I can prevent it if that's at all possible. What panics me is when I realise that I can't prevent it; then what do I do?

I hide my disability. The only people who know I have autism are my close friends and family, no-one else I know online or have met in clubs or groups weren't told. I don't like the thought of being seen in a way that doesn't fit who I am before I've had the chance to get to know someone because there seems to be a lot of misinformation out there. I don't feel safe being autistic because people rarely understand what being autistic means so I'm afraid people will make a snap judgement about who I am based on the limited information they may have on one or two people they know with autism, or even worse—assumptions from television or films. The truth is, we might all have autism, but we are all different. There are certain triggers which I believe we often share, but how we deal with those triggers depends on who we are, where on the spectrum we roll and our past experiences. Not only that but some days I cope better than others.

I have been invited to speak to people online, but I don't want to because it could either go really well or 99 million ways wrong. It would be nice to have a verbal conversation sometimes instead of relying on text chat in the group, but I'm afraid to because I'm sure they think I'm in my twenties and I feel respected. I don't want anyone to know I'm much younger and start treating me differently.

It would hurt me to be thought of negatively or treated like a child, especially when I feel so much older than I am. This is me overthinking, I know, but I can't help it.

I won't ride out on my motorbike sometimes because I'm not feeling socially confident and I'm afraid that if I had an accident or someone bumped into me, I wouldn't be able to deal with it.

I worry about going out when it's not necessary—for example, when I'm going out just to enjoy a ride on my bike—because I think if anything happened and I got into an accident, it would be my own fault for leaving the house when I didn't need to.

If my mum asks me to get something in for dinner, then I feel justified in taking the bike out and taking the risk. I know this may seem silly—my mum encourages me to go out and enjoy myself, especially on sunny days—but I can't avoid it. I overthink and talk myself out of it.

I pre-empt worry and figure out a solution to any fear I can think of.

I've been worried about riding too slow on a 40-mph road on my 50cc motorbike and actually have my motorcycle training instructor on speed dial in case I'm stopped by a police officer and told I'm going dangerously slow up a hill... Sometimes I can't get higher than 20 mph. My speed dial is prepared so I can say to the officer that my instructor said it was legal for me to ride on the road and prove it with a phone call. Intellectually, I know I'm legal, but it feels so dangerous to me to ride so slow on the road that I can't help worrying about it.

Then there are those evenings when I'm trying to

sleep, and my brain says 'nope!'

My mind runs at a thousand miles an hour, and I worry about not waking up on time and having to be somewhere. I can't force myself to sleep, I have to listen to music, learn a language (currently Spanish), and try to exhaust myself until I eventually become too tired to stay awake.

Sleep has been a problem for me for as long as I can remember.

When I wake naturally, I'm okay, but I never wake up to an alarm. My alarm wakes the whole house several times before I'll stir. My mum has had long conversations with me, not realising I'm still fast asleep, and now has to encourage me out of bed before I'll feel alert.

I can get up feeling exhausted when I have to be somewhere and then fill my day with activity after activity, but no matter how physically or mentally tired I am, I still find it difficult to switch my brain off. I will sit in bed in the dark for hours listening to music until either I fall asleep, or I get up and start doing something productive.

What has helped me!

- ✓ Talking about what's on my mind.
- ✓ Accepting it and trying to focus on something else.
- ✓ Learning to stay calm when I can't sleep.
- ✓ Accepting that I'm doing the best I can.

Overthinking Notes

Write what helps you!

SENSORY CHALLENGES

I've spoken about how difficult it is for me to
vocalise my feelings and emotions. Sensory
difficulties for me usually have the same effect.
I'm getting better at identifying problems as I get
older, but at times if I feel too cold, too hot, I'm
hungry, thirsty or need the bathroom, this won't
reach my brain until the very last minute.

So, I'm never just a bit hungry—I'm starving, or
I'm too full because I haven't realised I've already
eaten enough, or I need the bathroom urgently
because it's taken me a long time to process that I

need to go. This often led to problems when I was a child.

Now I recognize when I'm getting triggered by things, like bright lights at night in a supermarket, especially when it's dark outside, and it's an extreme change from dark to fluorescent light.

Auditory intrusions hurt my ears. In the cinema, I dislike the level of noise coming through the speakers behind me, and I feel the vibrations throughout my whole body. Bright lights, the sound of fluorescent lighting, loud music in shops or restaurants, the sun when it's bright, and clothes with the tags left inside or made of scratchy material will drive me to distraction.

I need to be able to wear cool, light-fitting clothes which are comfortable, and I use layers throughout the day to help me regulate my body temperature.

Even in the summer I usually wear my hoodie

because I like to be able to hide inside the hood. More recently, I sometimes keep my motorbike helmet on because I like the privacy it gives me and the message it sends that I don't want to start a conversation with anyone. On my bad days, I keep my helmet on when I'm walking the dog.

I like food to be consistent. Cold food from the fridge and hot food to be eaten while it's still hot. Food must be served the way I'm expecting, it must be fresh, not touching other foods on the plate, and cooked the same way I'm expecting it to be cooked every time otherwise I lose my appetite or struggle to eat it, I'm not sure why.

As a child, the sound of the knife or fork scraping the plate was a problem for me, although I don't struggle with it as much now.

Background chatter and noise are painful for me. I can't concentrate on anything people are saying if there's a lawnmower on in the distance or if there's someone working on a construction site with loud machines nearby. The scraping of chairs over the wooden floor and the scratch of chalk down a board sets me on edge. My earphones and listening to music often help me with these distractions. Still, there are times when people accuse me of not listening or not engaging because I'm finding the auditory surroundings too much for me to cope with.

When I'm in a coffee shop, I will hear absolutely everything: the clinking of cutlery, every conversation, machines making coffee and staff calling to each other. If anyone tries to have a conversation with me during these times, I'll nod but usually haven't heard a word of what they've said.

 I haven't needed to put my hands over my ears because of it yet, but I've been close to it many times.

My bedding must be recently washed and smell clean, if it isn't, it drives me crazy.

Sometimes, I can't face getting wet. As a child, I

went through stages of loving the water and enjoying a daily bath before bedtime, and then suddenly I wouldn't want to get wet. I didn't like the feel of having wet hair and didn't want to have to go through the sensory process of going from wet to dry.

However, there are many sensory things which gave me a lot of pleasure as a child. Bubbles, splashing in the water, watching things float and the sound of remote-control toys. Music that I liked, as long as it wasn't too loud, was a sensory delight too, and I loved toys that made a sound when you pressed buttons and pushed the ball down the chute, the smell of Play-Doh and the sensation of squidgy dough in my hands.

What has helped me!

- ✓ Checking for causes of sensory issues when I feel anxious or out of control.
- ✓ Taking off tags on my clothes.
- ✓ Being careful not to put myself in a situation where I would have to

experience a sudden sensory change, like going into a hot room from outside in the cold with a heavy jacket on, or walking into fluorescent light at night or from a much darker room.

Sensory Challenges Notes

Write what helps you!

APPOINTMENTS

The hairdressers/barbers are a social nightmare for me. As a young boy, I let my hair grow really long because I wouldn't let my mum take me to the hairdressers.

I hate being stuck in a chair while someone I don't know is tugging at my head.

I have had the same hairdresser now for several years, and she is really nice, but still, I don't like it and have to force myself to go.

I'd rather suffer with long hair in the summer than go and get it cut. I was much better when we got our golden retriever puppy as a kid, because the hairdressers loved dogs and allowed us to bring him in with us. That made me feel a lot better because they talked about our dog and the focus was off me.

I never know what to talk about, say or do. I usually just sit there and say nothing, but thankfully our hairdresser knows me now and knows I have autism.

I don't like going to appointments when I don't know what to expect. I have to know everything that will happen. I feel anxious because I don't feel comfortable asking questions. When you're a kid people often assume, you're going to comply with whatever they say, and that you're not interested in knowing why they've asked you to do something. This is true of the dentist. When I had fluoride paste put on my teeth it drove me nuts, it was bitty in my mouth, and I had to scrape it all off the second I got out of there. As simple as it might sound, just being asked step by step if I'm okay with what is going to happen next gives me the confidence that I need to feel safe in that environment. I feel more in control and respected. As I get older, I realise I'm going to have to start filling in forms, and the idea of that scares me because I feel like I'm going to fill the form out wrong or misunderstand the questions and end up looking like an idiot. One of the worst things about the doctors is having to sit in a large waiting room with everyone else.

Going inside a busy surgery and having to talk to a doctor that I don't know makes me anxious because I don't feel comfortable talking to people I don't know, whatever their profession.

Where I live, it's tough to get to see the same doctor every time. Usually, you get an appointment with whoever is available, so unless I'm forced to go, I won't. I'm lucky, apart from autism I'm healthy, so I've only ever had to go a couple of times in my life. But when I have, my mum has done all the talking, because I don't like talking about my issues to someone I don't know. Sometimes it takes me a while to decide to discuss things with my mum, so there's no hope of me feeling comfortable with a doctor I don't know. My mum made an appointment recently because she wanted to find out if there were any medications, I could take to help me with my anxiety to see if it would make me feel confident enough to take exams.

I don't like taking pills, even just over-the-counter pills; I refuse to take them unless I feel I really can't take the pain anymore. I prefer to use cognitive behavioural therapy, CBD spray, a good comedy on Netflix or mindfulness as a strategy to calm myself down, or better still, not put myself in a situation I'm not able to cope with. I haven't taken the pills and I doubt I will, but I suppose they are good to have if I change my mind.

I had an interview with my local college to join a

course, and I thought I was going to wait outside the room until I was invited in with my mum to discuss the course and what was expected of me. That didn't happen, and there was no structure, just lots of different teaching staff coming in looking for people who'd registered for different courses, and we were taken through the college right to the other end of the building until we had no idea where we were.

At this point I was already on the brink of a meltdown. Then I found out groups of people were being called in at once, I wasn't expecting that, and I had to leave. I've never been alone at any appointment, and right now I can't imagine a time when I would feel comfortable going to any of these appointments by myself. I hope that changes as I get older.

What has helped me!

- ✓ Preparing for appointments ahead of time and talking through what's expected.

✓ Having an advocate with me to explain my difficulties when I can't.

✓ Building trust and having continuity of care, whenever possible.

✓ Accepting that there are times when I have to leave, no matter how much I'd like to stay, because it's better to prevent myself from having a crisis than to push myself over the edge.

Appointments Notes

Write what helps you!

LITERAL /VISUAL THINKING

It took a long time for me to realise that what people said wasn't always what they meant.

I often don't understand what is meant to be a joke and automatically translate communication into a literal meaning. As I've gotten older, I've become better at this, but I don't get hints most of the time, so I need explicit instruction and honest emotional dialogue to connect with friends and family.

I learned a lot more about idioms and irony studying English and that was interesting, but sometimes in practice, I can forget. It doesn't click straight away, which can cause me a lot of confusion.

It's much easier if people just say what they mean instead of trying to give hints because I won't get it, and often this results in an upset from people who've thought I should know what they 'really' mean when I don't.

This is another problem with being so able as a person on the spectrum, because I am aware that in every other way I look and sound like someone my age who doesn't have a disability, but I do. My mind works differently, and it can be extremely frustrating at times.

To give some examples:

In a nutshell—I see a nut inside its shell.

Bless her cotton socks—I imagine God blessing a woman wearing cotton socks.

Pull your socks up—I imagine someone pulling

their socks up.

Raining cats and dogs—I imagine cartoon cats and dogs falling onto the street from the sky.

Sleep on it—I see a bed.

I understand these idioms now, but when I was little, they were incredibly confusing.

Sometimes adults have threatened extreme violence in word, but this has been a 'joke' that everyone else has laughed at.

For someone on the spectrum yet to learn about this kind of dialogue, this is damaging and extremely frightening, especially for someone young.

I remember a family member seeing my little brother take a piece of food from the kitchen. He turned to him and said 'little boys who take food without asking will have their fingers cut off,' and he gestured to the electric carving knife he was holding in his hand.

This was just a joke, and he was upset when he realized the terror my brother experienced as a result, but my brother fell into a meltdown nonetheless.

My imagination is acute. If I'm eating and someone mentions anything unpleasant at the table, I will imagine the image in my head immediately, and that will put me off my food. I have left food I was enjoying and gone hungry many times before when I've been put off by something someone has said at the dinner table.

When I think, I think in pictures, so if I need to remember something, I need a visual cue. This often also means that when people are talking to me, I can't process information the way people would like me to. If I'm given directions verbally, I'm more likely to forget everything I've been told than if I'm given them written down so that I can see them written down and create a picture in my mind.

What has helped me!

- ✓ Explaining to friends and family how I think.
- ✓ Having my feelings validated when I've become distressed because of a misunderstanding in communication.
- ✓ Learning through visualisation.
- ✓ Asking for instructions to be written down clearly.

Visual / Literal Thinking Notes

Write what helps you!

UNEXPECTED SITUATIONS

I recently had a meltdown in a restaurant with my dad and my brother. I ordered a non-dairy pizza, and it came with dairy cheese. I could tell from the smell as soon as it was brought to the table.

The staff apologised, took it away and replaced it with another one, but because a mistake was made, I wondered how many other errors might have been made that I couldn't see.

I started overthinking and considered whether

the pizza was actually going to be fresh, or whether they'd just scraped the dairy off and replaced it with a non-dairy version. I couldn't clear my mind of worry, and I really didn't want to eat after that because I didn't trust the service and I overthought everything like I often do.

They brought me another pizza, but I was unable to eat it, even though I was assured it was a new pizza. I left it, and as soon as my family had finished their meals, I wanted to go, but they decided to order dessert, and I didn't want to order anything else. I felt myself starting to slip into a meltdown.

I wish I knew why. I don't understand the reason behind it, but at times like these, I have to take myself away from the situation physically to be able to think. I have to reset my brain to the moment before everything started going wrong, and process. In this case, I jumped over the seat and left the restaurant.

Feeling out of control like this makes me tense

and frustrated, and often moving away from the situation calms me down. I can deal with it better after time away to process and think more logically by getting out of my emotional brain.

Now when I think back on the situation, I see how strange it was. I ask myself why, why did I react like that? I could have just not eaten the pizza... I'm not an unreasonable person, but situations like these overwhelm me in that particular moment. I lose trust, and then I lose the ability to remain in that situation. I have a fight or flight response, and for me, it always results in me going into flight mode.

This reaction isn't something I can control yet, but it is something I'm working on.

I've already talked about how unexpected social interaction and communication makes me feel, whether that's phone calls, a knock on the door or letters, etc.... Anything unexpected can be a trigger for my anxiety.

In the past, I have been in situations where I've unexpectedly found myself within a group of people I didn't know very well, and I wondered what I was doing there. It could have been because my brother and I had been outside and a group of kids had come up to speak to us, or within an organized activity where more people joined us who I'd never met, but whatever the reason, it threw me and made me feel unsure of myself, confused and anxious.

In these situations, I don't know what to do, say, or how to act. I often shut down and follow the group. Growing up, this sometimes led to me being thought of as a quiet, shy kid, but it's never a pleasant experience for me.

As a child, I would have major problems if there were any changes in plan, especially if it was at the last minute and I had been looking forward to something. Even just having something for dinner I hadn't expected could make me sad and anxious. If something was served in a way which wasn't what I was used to, it made me feel very uneasy and unsafe. As I've grown, this isn't so bad because I've learned to understand my reaction and can see it more logically, but from a child's eyes, it's devastating when there's any change, even if it's something really silly and seemingly small to everyone else.

What has helped me!

- ✓ Explaining to family and friends that I don't mean to come across as disrespectful or dramatic when I feel out of control. By taking myself away from a situation, I'm taking steps to regain control so I can recover my equilibrium without going into a full-blown meltdown, shutdown or panic attack.

- ✓ I've learned to tell people I'm with how I will react if I'm not expecting additional people to join us. It isn't that I don't want to be sociable, it's just that I need time to adjust to unexpected changes in plans.

Unexpected Situations Notes

Write what helps you!

SPECIAL INTERESTS

You may have heard that people on the spectrum have special interests – interests which become more of an obsession. In my case, it's true.

Thomas the Tank Engine was my first special interest.

All my puzzles and games featured trains from the books. My parents took me to Thomas's Day Out a few times, where they'd take me on a steam train which was made to look like Thomas, and we met the Fat Controller.

My wallpaper was a Thomas the Tank Engine design; so was my bedding and most of my clothes, toys and anything else I could find.

It wasn't long after that I discovered wheels, and I realised how much I loved cars. Most people say all boys love cars or anything with wheels, but I would choose to spend every free second I had drawing cars, playing with toy cars, riding in cars, spotting cars, counting cars...you get the point. For me, it was all about realism.

The cars had to look like the full-size version; I wanted cars that had headlights and mats with roads that were identical to UK roads, with the correct lines and rules of the road, and spaces large enough to fit my toy cars on precisely.

I wouldn't let my brother steer his car around the roundabout the wrong way.

I've often told my mum I wanted to build a company which made toy cars with headlights and better road play mats for kids on the spectrum. I still might.

So, I've loved cars since I was very young, and anything related to that topic will always interest me. I talk my mum to death about cars, whether it's the one I want when I'm older, a brand new one I spot on the road, or foreign cars. Yes, I love to check out the number plates to find out where they've come from; I'm always happy to talk about cars!

What has helped me!

- ✓ I have learned to understand that not everyone wants to hear me talk for hours about my special interests, so I try to warn people ahead of time that I might not be easily silenced if the subject comes up.

Special Interests Notes
Write what helps you!

GOOD DAYS AND BAD

Some days I feel on top of the world. My confidence is at an all-time high and I think I could commit to anything at all, whether that's socialising, staying overnight at a family house, speaking on the phone, whatever. But when reality kicks in and I'm actually expected to do it, it's an entirely different story.

I feel bad when I commit to things and then realise I really can't do it, especially if it's at the last minute. I know my mum was really excited when I said I'd go to college and do a mechanics course.

What she didn't know is that as soon as we got home from the open day, I had reservations and was anxious every time I thought about it.

At the interview, when everything went wrong, it confirmed my belief that I wasn't ready to put myself in a situation I didn't feel prepared to deal with. When we first discussed it and I met the tutors, I genuinely thought it was something I was capable of doing because at that time it was nine months away, which seemed like forever; but forever came around much quicker than I had expected!

It's not unusual for me to genuinely believe that I can do something until I'm struck with the reality, and it's just as upsetting for me as it is for my family. I want to do all the things other kids my age do.

I want to be able to enjoy college life and have

friends, talk about common interests and do well academically. I want to be able to take exams and show my family what I'm capable of, but it feels impossible for me, and it knocks my confidence.

Some days I do well, I have a plan, and I stick to it, and nothing seems to get in the way. But other days it feels as if nothing goes right, the smallest thing interrupts my flow, and it feels like a domino effect. Only one thing has to fall out of place for my whole day to feel as though it's imploding, and I have no way to control it.

I enjoy helping other people and often offer to help edit videos or do chores, but sometimes I regret it when I'm not I the right frame of mind because I hate letting people down.

What has helped me!

- ✓ I've learned not to make promises on the days when I'm feeling super confident, to prevent letting people down.
- ✓ Understanding that my disability is often

hidden and that on good days, people may not believe I have autism at all because I can come across so well.

✓ Not being made to feel bad when I can't fulfil a plan I made on a good day because I'm having a bad one.

Good Days & Bad Notes

Write what helps you!

CONCLUSION

Autism is a spectrum and no two people on the autism spectrum experience their ASD in the same way, but as individual as we are, we share the need to feel respected, understood and valued for the gifts we have.

Ed from the charitable organisation 'Autistica' mentioned in a recent email that Curtin University in Australia and the Karolinska Institute in Sweden say certain strengths are as important to consider as challenges when discussing autism, including:

- ✓ Attention to detail.
- ✓ Visual perception.
- ✓ Memory.
- ✓ Creative and artistic talents.
- ✓ Mathematical and technical abilities.
- ✓ Interests or expertise in 'niche' areas.
- ✓ Character strengths like honesty and loyalty.

CRISIS & HELPFUL PEOPLE

Make a note of at least two people who have told you they want you to reach out to them if you need support. These are the people who WANT to be there for you.

It's okay to ask for help ~ you would want them to contact you if they needed you.

Name

Number

Name

Number

If you don't want to talk to someone you know, why not speak to someone you don't?

In the United Kingdom - Autism Helpline: Telephone: 0808 800 4104

The Samaritans: 116 123

IF YOU HAVE THOUGHTS OF SUICIDE OR SELF-HARM PLEASE SEEK HELP NOW!

In a crisis?

Text **HOME** to connect with a Crisis Counselor. **Free 24/7 support at your fingertips.**

UK: text 85258 | Ireland: text 50808

US and Canada: text 741741

How It Works

Text HOME from anywhere, anytime. Crisis Text Line is here for any crisis. A live, trained Crisis Counselor receives the text and responds, all from our secure online platform. The volunteer Crisis Counselor will help you move from a hot moment to a cool moment.

More Information: UK

The National Autistic Society 393 City Road, London, EC1V 1NG, United Kingdom. [Administrative offices only] Tel: +44 (0)20 7833 2299 Fax: +44 (0)20 7833 9666. Email: nas@nas.org.uk

ABOUT THE AUTHOR

Callum Knight lives with his family in Kent, UK. If you have any questions, you can reach him at: thesecretsofmyspectrum@gmail.com

MORE FROM FRAMI BOOKS

17-year-old Ariessy must learn to accept her weakness, as well as her power if she is going to survive.

"A fast-paced, fantasy adventure with a strong and relatable protagonist. Highly recommended!"
- **The Wishing Shelf**

Find out more at Framibooks.com.

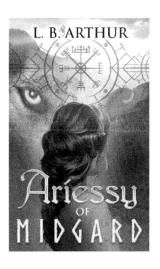

Printed in Great Britain
by Amazon

17642921R00081